Instant MDX Queries for SQL Server 2012

Learn how to write MDX queries from SQL Server Analysis Services 2012 cubes quickly and easily

Nicholas Emond

BIRMINGHAM - MUMBAI

Instant MDX Queries for SQL Server 2012

Copyright © 2013 Packt Publishing

All rights reserved. No part of this book may be reproduced, stored in a retrieval system, or transmitted in any form or by any means, without the prior written permission of the publisher, except in the case of brief quotations embedded in critical articles or reviews.

Every effort has been made in the preparation of this book to ensure the accuracy of the information presented. However, the information contained in this book is sold without warranty, either express or implied. Neither the author, nor Packt Publishing, and its dealers and distributors will be held liable for any damages caused or alleged to be caused directly or indirectly by this book.

Packt Publishing has endeavored to provide trademark information about all of the companies and products mentioned in this book by the appropriate use of capitals. However, Packt Publishing cannot guarantee the accuracy of this information.

First published: August 2013

Production Reference: 1230813

Published by Packt Publishing Ltd.
Livery Place
35 Livery Street
Birmingham B3 2PB, UK.

ISBN 978-1-78217-806-4

www.packtpub.com

Cover Image by Aniket Sawant (aniket_sawant_photography@hotmail.com)

Credits

Author
Nicholas Emond

Reviewers
Phuong Dao
Derek Evans
Moustafa Refaat

Acquisition Editor
Akram Hussain

Commissioning Editor
Priyanka Shah

Technical Editors
Anita Nayak
Sampreshita Maheshwari

Project Coordinator
Suraj Bist

Proofreader
Lesley Harrison

Production Coordinator
Manu Joseph

Graphics
Abhinash Sahu

Cover Work
Manu Joseph

About the Author

Nicholas Emond has been working in Information Technologies for the last eleven years. His past jobs were as a programmer with VB.NET, administrator of a corporate SharePoint intranet and business intelligence developer when he started to use the Microsoft BI stack since SQL Server 2005. Currently, he is a business intelligence consultant working in Montreal, Canada. Nicholas has certifications in Microsoft SQL Server and Microsoft SharePoint and he is a Competent Communicator from Toastmasters International. He likes to read books on computing and personal growth. MDX Queries for SQL Server 2012 Starter is the first book written by Nicholas Emond, and it won't be his last.

Ce livre est dédié à Marie, Benjamin et Thomas. Je vous aime gros gros gros et fort fort fort. Je vous aime gros comme le ciel, et le ciel, c'est GROS!

> I would like to thank my wonderful wife for her encouragement and support while working on this book. I would like to thank my parents; it's because of you that I'm what I am today. A big "Thanks" to my friends— Phuong, David, Samir, Mohammad, Nicolas, Alexandre, Martine, and Kiet for believing in me and showing me that writing a book would be a great experience for me. To Aurita D'souza from Packt Publising, thank you for asking me on About.me if I would like to write a book on MDX queries. Priyanka Shah and Suraj Bist, also from Packt Publishing, I had a great time working with you.

About the Reviewers

Phuong Dao has over thirteen years of experience in application and data warehouse development for the pharmaceutical, financial, distribution, manufacturing, and telecommunication sectors. He held various positions as analyst, team leader and developer in business intelligence and application projects. Recently, he acted as a Business Intelligence developer in a financial company. He was responsible to develop and support two projects that were developed with the Microsoft BI tools, SQL Server, SSIS, SSAS, and SSRS. His experience over the years in development helped him build a solid background in completing the various projects he took part of. Mr. Dao's enthusiasm, drive, and versatility enable him to adapt quickly to new technologies and colleagues.

Derek Evans started out in the Microsoft world after getting out of college at Rochester Institute of Technology. He got his first job as Tech Support rep at Keyspan Energy (Brooklyn Union and Gas) supporting their customer support system. At Keyspan Derek supported Keyspan in the transition from Microsoft Access 95 to SQL 6.5 and SQL 2000. He learned hands on how to design databases using SQL Server 2000 and how to integrate systems using Data Transformation Services. He is now a consultant with NextEra Energy doing Energy Trading BI using SQL 2012 Analysis Services Multidimensional and Tabular data cubes.

Moustafa Refaat has over fifteen years of experience developing software solutions, leading the architecture, design, coding, and refactoring of many large projects.

Some of the organizations he worked with include the City of Vaughan, TransCanada Pipelines, Tim Horton's, VMS, Deloitte DMGF, Newfoundland and Labrador, and First Canadian Title Insurance. Moustafa has designed and implemented many systems based on SQL Server and BizTalk. His experience span the industries of Financial, Insurance, Health, Banking, Retail, Oil and Gas, Marketing and Telecommunications services automation.

He is a published author with books on programming, and BizTalk. He also acted as a referee for the IEEE Software magazine. Moustafa runs his own software and consulting company; Genetic Thought Inc.

www.packtpub.com

Support files, eBooks, discount offers and more

You might want to visit `www.packtpub.com` for support files and downloads related to your book.

Did you know that Packt offers eBook versions of every book published, with PDF and ePub files available? You can upgrade to the eBook version at `www.packtpub.com` and as a print book customer, you are entitled to a discount on the eBook copy. Get in touch with us at `service@packtpub.com` for more details.

At `www.packtpub.com`, you can also read a collection of free technical articles, sign up for a range of free newsletters and receive exclusive discounts and offers on Packt books and eBooks.

packtlib.packtpub.com

Do you need instant solutions to your IT questions? PacktLib is Packt's online digital book library. Here, you can access, read and search across Packt's entire library of books.

Why Subscribe?
- Fully searchable across every book published by Packt
- Copy and paste, print and bookmark content
- On demand and accessible via web browser

Free Access for Packt account holders

If you have an account with Packt at www.packtpub.com, you can use this to access PacktLib today and view nine entirely free books. Simply use your login credentials for immediate access.

Table of Contents

Instant MDX Queries for SQL Server 2012 — 1

So, what is MDX for SQL Server 2012? — 3
Installation — 5
Step 1 – identify which edition to use — 5
- The Developer edition — 5
- The Evaluation edition — 5
- 32-bit or 64-bit — 5
Step 2 – review the requirements — 5
Step 3 – downloading the SQL Server 2012 trial edition — 5
Step 4 – installing the SQL Server 2012 — 6
Step 5 – installing the Data Warehouse — 8
Step 6 – installing the multidimensional models — 8
And that's it — 9
Quick start – writing your first MDX query — 10
Step 1 – open the SQL Server Management Studio and connect to the cube — 10
Step 2 – SELECT — 11
- Axes — 11
- Tuples — 12
- Sets — 12
Step 3 – FROM — 13
Step 4 – WHERE — 14
Step 5 – comments — 14
Step 6 – your first MDX query — 14
Top 4 features you'll want to know about — 16
Using functions — 16
- Basic keywords and functions — 16
- It's all in the family — 21
- Can you spare the time? — 24

Table of Contents

Using Calculated Members and Named Sets — 25
- Calculated Members — 25
- Named Sets — 27

Calculations — 27
- The calculation tab — 28
- Add a new Calculated Member — 28
- Add a new Named Set — 29

Writing for SSRS — 29
- Create a Report Project — 30
- Create a new report — 30
- Create a data source — 30
- Create a dataset — 31
- Create a table — 33
- The Months parameter — 34

DMVs — 37

People and places you should get to know — 39
- Official Sites — 39
- Articles and Tutorials — 39
- Blogs — 39
- Twitter — 40

Instant MDX Queries for SQL Server 2012

Welcome to the MDX Queries for SQL Server 2012. This book has been especially created to provide you with all the information that you need to get setup with MDX Queries for SQL Server 2012. You will learn the basics of MDX, get started with installing SQL Server 2012, building your first MDX query, and discover some tips and tricks for writing MDX queries.

This document contains the following sections:

So, what is MDX Queries for SQL Server 2012? – In this section you will find out what MDX actually is, what you can do with it, and why it's so great.

Installation – In this section you will learn how to install SQL Server 2012 with the minimum fuss and then set it up so that you can use it as soon as possible.

Quick start – This section will show you how to perform one of the core tasks of MDX; writing queries. Follow the steps to write your own query, which will be the basis of most of your work in MDX for SQL Server 2012.

Top 4 features you need to know about – In this section you will learn how to perform four tasks with the most important features of MDX. By the end of this section, you will be able to write MDX queries, use MDX functions, write calculations and KPIs, and to write queries to get your cube documentation.

People and places you should get to know – This section provides you with many useful links to the pages and forums, as well as a number of helpful articles, tutorials, blogs, and the Twitter feeds of MDX super-contributors.

So, what is MDX for SQL Server 2012?

The **MDX** or **Multidimensional Expressions** is a query language used to retrieve data inside the Microsoft SQL Server Analysis Services cubes such as those built with the **Microsoft SQL Server 2012**. With MDX, you can display the elements of your cube, such as attributes and hierarchies from your dimensions, measures from your fact tables, calculations, and KPIs. Here's a list of client applications where you can write MDX or where MDX is used behind the scenes:

- **Excel**: When you design `PivotTables` and `PivotCharts`, Excel is querying the SQL Server Analysis Services cubes using the MDX.
- **Reporting Services Reports**: The **SQL Server Reporting Services** (**SSRS**) reports are based on cubes have queries and are written in MDX.
- **PerformancePoint Dashboards**: These are created in PerformancePoint Dashboard with the SSAS data sources are sending the MDX queries to retrieve the data to be displayed in scorecards.
- **SQL Server Data Tools**: This is the application to design reports and cubes. For the cubes, you can write MDX to define Calculations, KPIs, Actions, and Securities.
- **SQL Server Management Studio**: This is used to write the MDX queries against the **SQL Server Analysis Services (SSAS)** cubes.

A multidimensional cube is composed of the following elements:

- Measures
- Dimensions
- Aggregates

Let's say that you want to know how many mountain bikes did my department did sell during May in Canada?. Measures are numbers, the answer to your question comes in the form of values. It's the how many sold part. With measures, you can show the sum, the average, minimum or maximum, or perform calculations on them to have other measures. They are stored in fact tables. Dimensions are the entry point into the cube, specific parts of your question such as mountain bikes (products dimension), my department (salesperson dimension), last month (time dimension), in Canada (geography dimension). Aggregations are values at upper levels of measures defined at the lower levels of the related dimensions. Here's an example of sales aggregated during the month of May for North-America from Canada, United States, and Mexico.

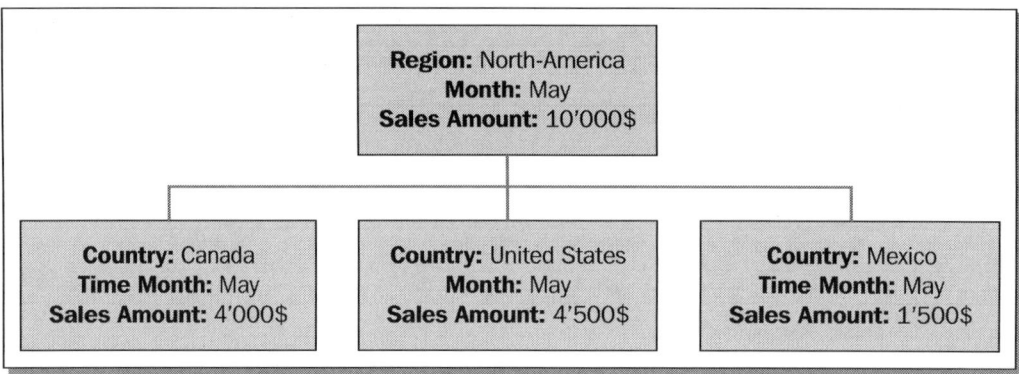

With MDX, you can write queries to retrieve the sales amount of the last month, only for Canada or for North-America, and the countries inside North-America.

Installation

In six easy steps, you can install the SQL Server 2012 and get it set up on your system. The Microsoft SQL Server 2012 comes in many flavors called editions.

Step 1 – identify which edition to use

Standard, Enterprise, Developer, or the new Business Intelligence, SQL Server 2012 comes in different editions. You can have a look of the editions at http://technet.microsoft.com/en-us/library/ms144275.aspx and read the supported features by editions there: http://technet.microsoft.com/en-us/library/cc645993.aspx. For development purposes, go for the Developer edition. If you want to test, the Evaluation edition is the best choice.

The Developer edition

The Developer edition includes all the functionality of the Enterprise edition. Be aware that it is licensed for development use only; it is not to be used in production. If you don't have the Developer edition available, you can download the Evaluation edition. Here is the link if you want to buy the Developer edition: http://www.microsoft.com/en-us/sqlserver/get-sql-server/how-to-buy.aspx.

The Evaluation edition

Like the Developer edition, the Evaluation edition includes all the functionality of the Enterprise edition. The trial will expire automatically after six months. You can download it from http://www.microsoft.com/en-us/download/details.aspx?id=29066.

32-bit or 64-bit

Take note that SQL Server 32-bit works on a 64-bit machine, but a 64-bit SQL Server won't install on a 32-bit processor.

Step 2 – review the requirements

Before installing SQL Server 2012 on your machine, you should review the requirements and make sure that you meet them. You can review the list at http://technet.microsoft.com/en-us/ms143506.aspx.

Step 3 – downloading the SQL Server 2012 trial edition

1. Go to http://www.microsoft.com/en-us/download/details.aspx?id=29066.
2. Choose your language and click on the **Download** button.
3. Choose the download that you want and then click on **Next**.
4. Save the file on your computer.

Step 4 – installing the SQL Server 2012

1. From the selected media, execute `setup.exe`.
2. In the **SQL Server Installation Center** window, on the left menu, select **Installation**.
3. In the right pane, click on **New SQL Server stand-alone installation or add features to an existing installation**.

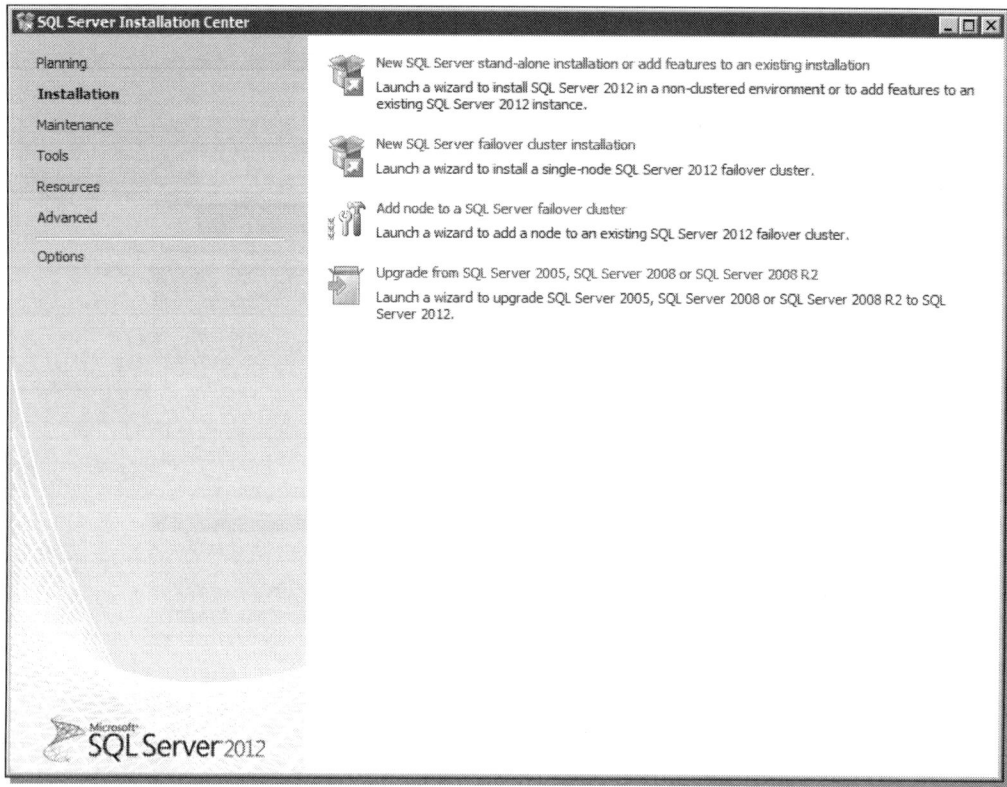

4. In the **Setup Support Rules** window, wait for the rules to validate and then click on **Next**.
5. If you encounter problems, correct them and then click on **Re-run** and then click on **Next**.
6. Enter a **Product Key** if you have to and then click on **Next**.
7. Select **I accept the license terms** and then click on **Next**.
8. If you have to, select **Include SQL Server product updates** and then click on **Next**.
9. Wait for the setup files to extract.
10. In the **Setup Support Rules** window, wait for the rules to validate and then click on **Next**.

11. If you encounter problems, correct them and then click on **Re-run** and then click on **Next**.
12. In the **Setup Role** window, select **SQL Server Feature Installation** and then click on **Next**.
13. In the **Feature Selection window**, you have to select at least the following:
    - Under Instance Features
        Database Engine Services
        Analysis Services
    - Under Shared Features
        SQL Server Data Tools
        Client Tools Connectivity
        Management Tools – Basic
        Management Tools – Complete
14. If you want to, you can change the directory for the **Shared feature directory and Shared feature directory (x86)** directories. Click on **Next**.
15. In the **Installation Rules** window, wait for the installation rules to validate and then click on **Next**.
16. If you encounter problems, correct them and then click on **Re-run** and then click on **Next**.
17. In the **Instance Configuration** window, you can select **Default instance** or **Named instance** and type a name for your instance. You can change the **Instance root directory**. When you are ready, click on **Next**.
18. Review the disk space requirements and then click on **Next**.
19. In the **Server Configuration** window, click on **Next**.
20. In the **Database Engine Configuration** window, click on **Add Current User** and then click on **Next**.
21. In the **Analysis Services Configuration** window, select **Multidimensional and Data Mining Mode**, click on **Add Current User**, and then click on **Next**.
22. In the **Error Reporting** window, if you want to send the SQL Server Error reports automatically to Microsoft, select **Send Windows and SQL Server Error Reports to Microsoft or your corporate report server**. Click on **Next**.
23. In the **Installation Configuration Rules** window, wait for the rules to validate and then click on **Next**. If you encounter problems, correct them and then click on **Re-run** and then click on **Next**.
24. In the **Ready to Install** window, click on **Install**.
25. Wait for the installation to finish and click on **Close**.

Step 5 – installing the Data Warehouse

A cube gets its data from a **Data Warehouse**. Data coming from various data sources have been extracted, cleaned, conformed, and delivered to the Data Warehouse. **CodePlex** provides the **AdventureWorks** Data Warehouse for SQL Server 2012. Here's how to get your hands on it.

1. Go to `http://msftdbprodsamples.codeplex.com/releases/view/55330`.
2. Click on the **AdventureWorksDW2012 Data File** link and download the MDF file.
3. You will find the instructions to attach the MDF file on the page `http://social.technet.microsoft.com/wiki/contents/articles/3735.sql-server-samples-readme.aspx` under the **Install AdventureWorksDW2012** section.

Step 6 – installing the multidimensional models

1. Go to `http://msftdbprodsamples.codeplex.com/releases/view/55330`.
2. Click on the **AdventureWorks Multidimensional Models SQL Server 2012** and download the ZIP file.
3. Extract the ZIP file, under the `Enterprise` folder, open the `AdventureWorksDW2012Multidimensional-EE.sln` file.
4. In Visual Studio, click on the **Project** menu, and then click on **Properties**. From the left menu, select **Deployment**.
5. On the right pane, under the **Target** section, type the server name in the **Server** textbox, and then click on **OK**.

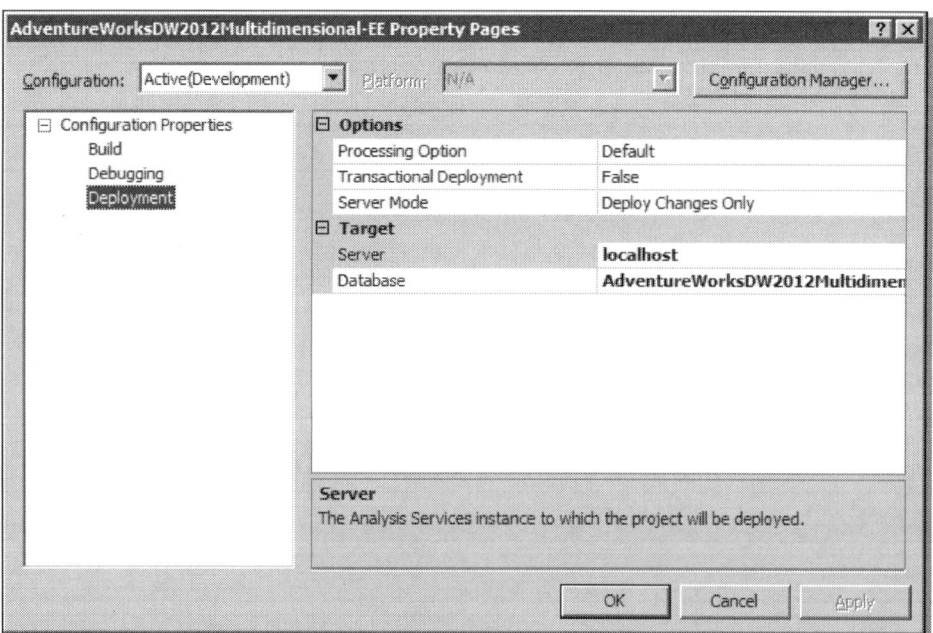

6. In the **Solution Explorer,** under **Data Sources,** double-click on `AdventureWorksDW2012.ds` and edit the connection string so that it connects on `AdventureWorksDW2012`. You may have to change the server name and the impersonation information.

7. In the **Solution Explorer,** right-click on **AdventureWorksDW2012Multidimensional-EE** and then click on **Process**.

8. If you see a window, **The server content appears to be out of date. Would you like to build and deploy the project first,** click on **Yes**.

9. Click on **Run,** click on **Close,** and then click on **Close**.

And that's it

By this point, you should have a working installation of the SQL Server 2012 and you are now free to play around and discover more about the MDX queries.

Quick start – writing your first MDX query

A MDX query is code and executed against a cube to have a result in a specific format return to the client application.

Step 1 – open the SQL Server Management Studio and connect to the cube

The **Microsoft SQL Server Management Studio (SSMS)** is a client application used by the administrators to manage instances and by developers to create object and write queries. We will use SSMS to connect on the cube and write our first MDX query. Here's a screenshot of SSMS with a connection on a SSAS server:

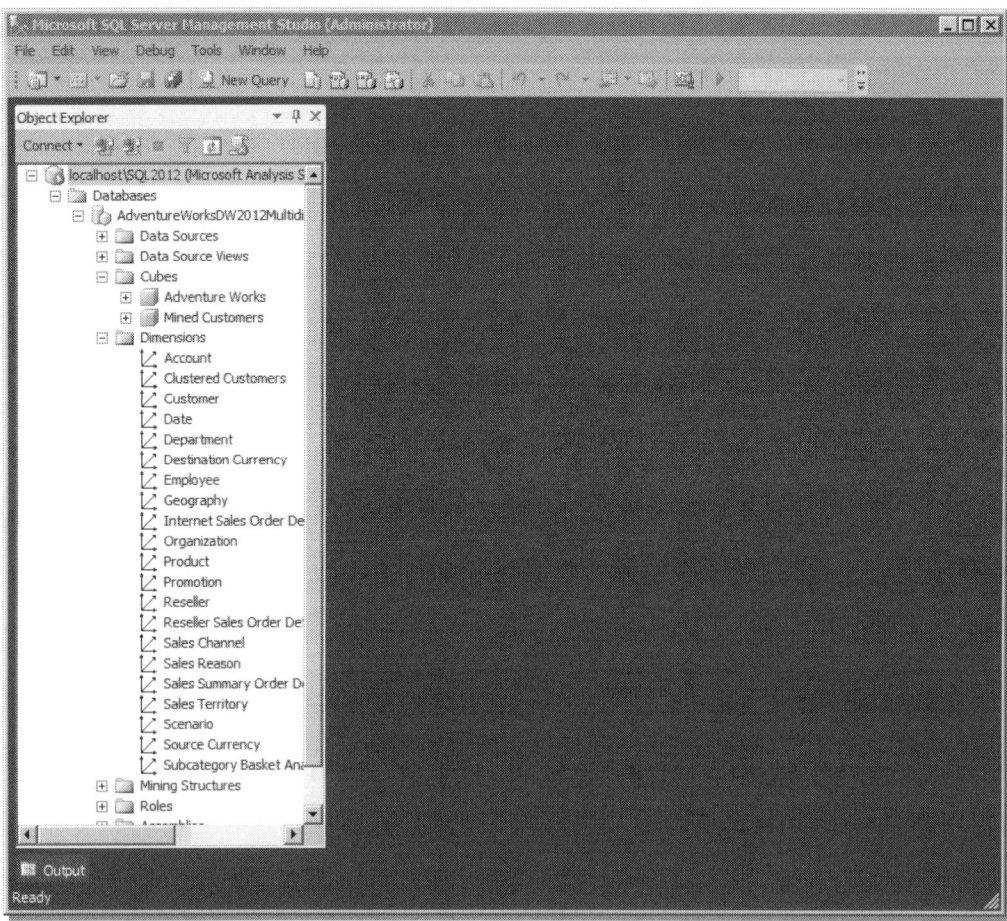

1. Click on the **Windows** button, click on **All Programs**, click on **Microsoft SQL Server 2012**, and then click on **SQL Server Management Studio**.
2. In the **Connect to Server** window, in the **Server type** box, select **Analysis Services**. In the **Server name** box, type the name of your Analysis Services server. Click on **Connect**.
3. In the **SQL Server Management Studio** window, click on the **File** menu, click on **New**, and then click on **Analysis Services MDX Query**.
4. In the **Connect to Analysis Services** window, in the **Server name** box, type the name of you Analysis Services server, and then click on **Connect**.
5. The basic MDX query contains the following three parts:
   - SELECT
   - FROM
   - WHERE

> If you have already written SQL queries, you might have already made connections with the **T-SQL** language. Here's my tip for you: don't, you will only hurt yourself. Some words are the same, but it is better to think MDX when writing MDX rather than to think SQL when writing MDX.

Step 2 – SELECT

The **SELECT** clause is the main part of the MDX query. You will define what are the measure and dimension members that you want to display. You also have to define on which axis of your result set you want to display the measure and dimension members.

Axes

Axes are the columns and rows of the result set. With SQL Server Analysis Services, upto 128 axes can be specified. The **axes** have a number which is zero-based. The first axe is 0, the second on is 1, and so on. So, if you want to use two axes, the first one will be 0 and the second will be 1. You cannot use axe 0 and axe 2, if you don't define axe 1. For the first five axes, you can use the axis alias instead. After the axe 4, you will have to revert to the number because no other aliases are available.

Axe Number	Alias
0	Columns
1	Rows
2	Pages
3	Sections
4	Chapters

> Even if SSAS supports 128 axes, if you try to use more than two axes in SSMS in your query, you will get this error when you execute your MDX query: `Results cannot be displayed for cellsets with more than two axes`. So, always write your MDX queries using only two axes in SSMS and separate them with a comma.

Tuples

A **tuple** is a specific point in the cube where dimensions meet. A tuple can contain one or more members from the cube's dimensions, but you cannot have two members from the same dimension. If you want to display only the calendar year 2008, you will have to write `[Date].[CY 2008]`. If you want to have more than one dimension, you have to enclose them using parenthesis `()` and separate them with a comma. Calendar year for United States will look like `([Date].[CY 2008], [Geography].[United States])`. Even if you are writing a tuple with only a single member from a single dimension, it is good practice to enclose it in parenthesis.

Sets

If you want to display the year 2005 to 2008, you will write four single-dimension tuples which composes a **set**. When writing the set, you separate the tuples with commas and wrap it all with curly braces `{}` and separate the tuples with commas such as `{ [Date].[CY 2005], [Date].[CY 2006] , [Date].[CY 2007] , [Date].[CY 2008] }` to have the calendar years from 2005 to 2008. Since all the tuples are from the same dimension, you can also write it using a colon (`:`), such as `{ [Date].[CY 2005] : [Date].[CY 2008] }` which will give you the years 2005 to 2008. With SSAS 2012, you can write `{ [Date].[CY 2008] : [Date].[CY 2005] }` and the result will still be from 2005 to 2008.

What about the calendar year 2008 for both Canada and the United States? You will write two tuples. A set can be composed of one or more tuples. The tuples must have the same dimensionality; otherwise, an error will occur. Meaning that the first member is from the `Date` dimension and the second from the `Geography` dimension. You cannot have the first tuple with `Date-Geography` and the second being `Geography-Date`; you will encounter an error. So the calendar year 2008 with Canada and United States will look such as `{ ([Date].[CY 2008], [Geography].[Canada]), ([Date].[CY 2008], [Geography].[United States]) }`.

When writing tuples, always use the form `[Dimension].[Level].[MemberName]`. So, `[Geography].[Canada]` should be written as `[Geography].[Country].[Canada]`. You could also use the member key instead of the member name. In SSAS, use the ampersand (`&`) when using the key; `[Geography].[State-Province].[Quebec]` with the name becomes `[Geography].[State-Province].&[QC]&[CA]` using the keys.

What happens when you want to write bigger sets such as for the bikes and components product category in Canada and the United States from 2005 to 2008? Enter the `Crossjoin` function. `Crossjoin` takes two or more sets for arguments and returns you a set with the cross products or the specified sets.

```
Crossjoin ({[Product].[Category].[Bikes], [Product].[Category].
[Components]}, {[Geography].[Country].[Canada], [Geography].[Country].
[United States]}, {[Date].[CY 2005] : [Date].[CY 2008]})
```

The MDX queries can be written using line-break to add visibility to the code. So each time we write a new set and even tuples, we write it on a new line and add some indentation:

```
Crossjoin (
   {
      [Product].[Category].[Bikes]
    , [Product].[Category].[Components]
   }
 ,
   {
      [Geography].[Country].[Canada]
    , [Geography].[Country].[United States]
   }
 , {[Date].[CY 2005] : [Date].[CY 2008]}
)
```

```
1   SELECT
2      {
3         [Measures].[Reseller Sales Amount]
4       , [Measures].[Reseller Order Quantity]
5      } on columns,
6      Crossjoin
7      (
8         {[Date].[CY 2006] : [Date].[CY 2008]}
9       ,
10        {
11           [Product].[Category].[Bikes]
12         , [Product].[Category].[Components]
13        }
14     ) on rows
```

Step 3 – FROM

The **FROM** clause defines where the query will get the data. It can be one of the following four things:

1. A cube.
2. A perspective (a subset of dimensions and measures).

3. A subcube (a MDX query inside a MDX query).
4. A dimension (a dimension inside your SSAS database, you must use the dollar sign ($) before the name of the dimension).

Step 4 – WHERE

The **WHERE** clause is used to filter the dimensions and members out of the MDX query. The set used in the WHERE clause won't be displayed in your result set.

```
FROM
     [Adventure Works]
WHERE
{
     [Geography].[Country].[Canada]
}
```

Step 5 – comments

Comment your code. You never know when somebody else will take a look on your queries and trying to understand what has been written could be harsh. There are three ways to use delimit comments inside the query:

1. /* and */
2. //
3. -- (pair of dashes)

The /* and */ symbols can be used to comment multiple lines of text in your query. Everything between the /* and the */ symbols will be ignored when the MDX query is parsed. Use // or -- to begin a comment on a single line.

Step 6 – your first MDX query

So if you want to display the `Resellers Sales Amount` and `Reseller Order Quantity` measures on the columns, the years from 2006 to 2008 with the bikes and components product categories for Canada. First, identify what will go where. Start with the two axes, continue with the FROM clause, and finish with the WHERE clause.

```
SELECT
{
[Measures].[Reseller Sales Amount]
, [Measures].[Reseller Order Quantity]
} on columns,
Crossjoin(
{ [Date].[CY 2006] : [Date].[CY 2008] }
```

```
, {
    [Product].[Category].[Bikes]
    , [Product].[Category].[Components]
  }
) on rows
FROM [Adventure Works]
WHERE { [Geography].[Country].[Canada] }
```

This query will return the following result set:

		Reseller Sales Amount	Reseller Order Quantity
CY 2006	Bikes	$3,938,283.99	4,563
CY 2006	Components	$746,576.15	2,954
CY 2007	Bikes	$4,417,665.71	5,395
CY 2007	Components	$997,617.89	4,412
CY 2008	Bikes	$1,909,709.62	2,209
CY 2008	Components	$370,698.68	1,672

```
/* Reseller Sales Amount and
Reseller Order Quantity per years 2006
and 2007 for Bikes and Components
Product Categories*/

SELECT
{

    [Measures].[Reseller Sales Amount]
    , [Measures].[Reseller Order Quantity]
} on columns,
Crossjoin
(
    {[Date].[CY 2006] : [Date].[CY 2008]}
    ,
    {
        [Product].[Category].[Bikes]
        , [Product].[Category].[Components]
    }
) on rows
FROM
    [Adventure Works]
WHERE
{
    [Geography].[Country].[Canada]
}
```

Top 4 features you'll want to know about

As you start to use the MDX Queries, you will realize that there are a wide variety of things that you can do with it. This section will teach you all about the most commonly performed tasks and most commonly used features in the MDX Queries.

The code used for the MDX queries are from the **AdventureWorks** cube installed in step 6 of the *Quick start* section.

Using functions

It won't take long for you to realize that you will need to write more than the basic MDX query. The MDX functions and operators are here to help you.

Basic keywords and functions

Basic keywords and functions are use when you need to do more with the MDX queries than just simply listing measure and dimension attributes.

- CrossJoin: The CrossJoin function takes two or more sets for arguments and returns a set with the cross products of the specified sets.

    CrossJoin (set1, set2, … set n)

- .members: Sometimes, instead of enumerating some members of a level, a hierarchy or all members of a dimension to compose your set, you might want all members. The .members operator will return all the members that you want. [Product].[Category].members will return **All Products, Accessories, Bikes, Clothing,** and **Components**.

    If you write [Product].[Category].[Category].members, you will get **Accessories, Bikes, Clothing,** and **Components** because you want all the member of the Product dimension from the Category attribute and at the Category level, which is [Product].[Category].[All Product]. The members under [Product].[Category].[All Product] are Accessories, Bikes, Clothing, and Components.

- Filter: Displaying all the members of one or more attributes is handy, but the first thing you will want to do, or somebody will ask you, is to filter the members out of another value. Here is the result of the following MDX query:

    ```
    select {[Measures].[Internet Sales Amount], [Measures].[Internet Order Count]} on 0,
    [Product].[Category].[Category].members on 1
    from [adventure works] where [Date].[Calendar].[Calendar Year].&[2008]
    ```

	Internet Sales Amount	Internet Order Count
Accessories	$407,050.25	10,657
Bikes	$9,162,324.85	5,805
Clothing	$201,524.64	4,451
Components	(null)	(null)

If you want to show the `Internet Sales Amount` where the `Internet Order Count` is higher than 5,000, you will use the `Filter` function. The first argument of the `Filter` function is the set to display. The second argument is a Boolean expression which if true for the evaluated member, it will be shown.

```
select {[Measures].[Internet Sales Amount]} on 0,
filter([Product].[Category].[Category].members, [Measures].
[Internet Order Count] >= 5000) on 1
from [adventure works] where [Date].[Calendar].[Calendar
Year].&[2008]
```

The preceding MDX query using the `filter` function returns:

	Internet Sales Amount
Accessories	$407,050.25
Bikes	$9,162,324.85

- **NON EMPTY**: The query to list the `Internet Order Count` for the categories in 2008 will look like this:

```
select {[Measures].[Internet Order Count]} on 0,
[Product].[Category].[Category].members on 1
from [adventure works] where [Date].[Calendar].[Calendar
Year].&[2008]
```

Here is the result of the Internet Order Count of the Product Categories in 2008:

	Internet Order Count
Accessories	10,657
Bikes	5,805
Clothing	4,451
Components	(null)

To get rid of the (null) of Components, you may use the NON EMPTY keyword. Once the query gets all the data, NON EMPTY removes the lines where all the columns are empty. You place NON EMPTY at the beginning of your axe like this:

```
select {[Measures].[Internet Order Count]} on 0,
non empty [Product].[Category].[Category].members on 1
from [adventure works] where [Date].[Calendar].[Calendar
Year].&[2008]
```

	Internet Order Count
Accessories	10,657
Bikes	5,805
Clothing	4,451

- NONEMPTY: The NONEMPTY function (written with no spaces) works like the NON EMPTY keyword, but with some minor differences. If you want to display both the Internet Order Count and the Order Count for all the Product categories in 2008 and using the NON EMPTY keyword, you will get this:

```
select {[Measures].[Internet Order Count], [Measures].[Order
Count]} on 0,
non empty [Product].[Category].[Category].members on 1
from [adventure works] where [Date].[Calendar].[Calendar
Year].&[2008]
```

	Internet Order Count	Order Count
Accessories	10,657	10,950
Bikes	5,805	6,529
Clothing	4,451	5,012
Components	(null)	601

Since there is at least one column with a value for all rows, the NON EMPTY returns all rows. To display rows where the Internet Order Count is not null, you will use the NONEMPTY function with your set to be displayed as the first argument. The second argument is one or more measures to evaluate and reject the rows, if they all the specified measures are empty.

So to get this:

	Internet Order Count	Order Count
Accessories	10,657	10,950
Bikes	5,805	6,529
Clothing	4,451	5,012

You will have to write this:

```
select {[Measures].[Internet Order Count], [Measures].[Order
Count]} on 0,
nonempty([Product].[Category].[Category].members, [Measures].
[Internet Order Count]) on 1
from [adventure works] where [Date].[Calendar].[Calendar
Year].&[2008]
```

- **Order**: Another basic MDX query request is to order the results. You can order the result of a query by using the Order function. The first argument is the set to order. The second argument is the value to order. It can be either a numeric or a string expression. The third optional argument is the sorting. The values for the sorting argument are ASC, DESC, BASC, and BDESC. ASC and DESC keep the hierarchy when sorting. BASC and BDESC break the hierarchy.

```
select {[Measures].[Order Count]} on 0,
order([Product].[Category].[Category].members, [Measures].[Order
Count], ASC) on 1
from [adventure works] where [Date].[Calendar].[Calendar
Year].&[2008]
```

The preceding code will return:

	Order Count
Components	601
Clothing	5,012
Bikes	6,529
Accessories	10,950

If we take the Order Count for all products by category in 2008 in descending order:

```
select {[Measures].[Order Count]} on 0,
non empty order(crossjoin([Product].[Category].[Category].members,
[Product].[Product].members), [Measures].[Order Count], DESC) on 1
from [adventure works] where [Date].[Calendar].[Calendar
Year].&[2008]
```

Here is the result (take note that a lot of rows have been taken out to enhance readability):

		Order Count
Accessories	All Products	10,950
Accessories	Water Bottle - 30 oz.	2,694
Accessories	Patch Kit/8 Patches	1,889

Accessories	Mountain Tire Tube	1,782
Bikes	All Products	6,529
Bikes	Mountain-200 Black, 38	416
Bikes	Road-750 Black, 52	391

Here is an example using the `BDESC` flag:

```
select {[Measures].[Order Count]} on 0,
non empty order(crossjoin([Product].[Category].[Category].members,
[Product].[Product].members), [Measures].[Order Count], BDESC) on 1
from [adventure works] where [Date].[Calendar].[Calendar Year].&[2008]
```

The result shows the `Order Count` in descending order mixing the `All Products` from the categories with the products. Here's a screenshot of a part of the result:

		Order Count
Accessories	All Products	10,950
Bikes	All Products	6,529
Clothing	All Products	5,012
Accessories	Water Bottle - 30 oz.	2,694
Accessories	Patch Kit/8 Patches	1,889
Accessories	Mountain Tire Tube	1,782
Clothing	AWC Logo Cap	1,504
Accessories	Sport-100 Helmet, Red	1,462
Accessories	Sport-100 Helmet, Blue	1,434
Accessories	Road Tire Tube	1,377
Accessories	Sport-100 Helmet, Black	1,352
Accessories	Fender Set - Mountain	1,238
Accessories	Mountain Bottle Cage	1,201
Accessories	Road Bottle Cage	1,005
Accessories	Touring Tire Tube	897
Accessories	HL Mountain Tire	816
Accessories	Bike Wash - Dissolver	706

- `Hierarchize`: The `Hierarchize` function takes a set as its first argument and optionally the `POST` keyword. The `POST` keyword will place the children first and the parent at the bottom of the list. Here is the `Hierarchize` function without `POST`:

```
select {[Measures].[Internet Order Count]} on 0,
non empty hierarchize(crossjoin([Product].[Category].&[1],
[Product].[Product].members)) on 1
from [adventure works] where [Date].[Calendar].[Calendar
Year].&[2008]
```

		Internet Order Count
Bikes	All Products	5,805
Bikes	Mountain-200 Black, 38	256
Bikes	Mountain-200 Black, 42	251
Bikes	Mountain-200 Black, 46	231
Bikes	Mountain-200 Silver, 38	254
...	...	...

Observe the `Hierarchize` function with the `POST` argument:

```
select {[Measures].[Internet Order Count]} on 0,
non empty hierarchize(crossjoin([Product].[Category].&[1],
[Product].[Product].members), POST) on 1
from [adventure works] where [Date].[Calendar].[Calendar
Year].&[2008]
```

		Internet Order Count
...	...	...
Bikes	Touring-3000 Yellow, 54	25
Bikes	Touring-3000 Yellow, 58	30
Bikes	Touring-3000 Yellow, 62	32
Bikes	All Products	5,805

It's all in the family

Members of a dimension compose a family. This includes the parent and the children. On a higher level, in a hierarchy, you have an ancestor and its descendants.

- ✦ `.parent`: The `.parent` function returns the parent on the upper level.

    The subcategory with ID 1 is `Mountain Bikes`. The parent of `Mountain Bikes` is `Bikes`.

    `[Product].[Product Categories].[Subcategory].&[1].parent`

- ✦ `.children`: The children of the `Mountain Bikes` product category are the products under the subcateogry `Mountain Bikes`.

    `[Product].[Product Categories].[Subcategory].&[1].children`

- **.nextmember:** The .nextmember function returns the next member in a given level. The next item after the Mountain Bikes subcategory is Road Bikes.

  [Product].[Product Categories].[Subcategory].&[1].nextmember

- **.prevmember:** The .prevmember function returns the previous member in a given level. The previous item before the Road Bikes subcategory is Mountain Bikes.

  [Product].[Product Categories].[Subcategory].&[2].prevmember

- **.lag():** The .lag() function is like the .prevmember function, but lag takes a number of step to get on the same level. Take note that you can supply a negative number making it a .lend() function.

  Here is a subset of the first members of the Product categories hierarchy of the Product dimension:

Level 1	Level 2	Level 3	Level 4
All Products	Category	Subcategory	Products
All Products	Accessories	Bike Racks	Hitch Rack – 4-Bike
		Bike Stands	All-Purpose Bike Stand
		Bottles and Cages	Mountain Bottle Cage
			Road Bottle Cage
			Water Bottle – 30 oz.

  A lend of 3 on the Hitch Rack - 4-Bike product is Road Bottle Cage.

- **.lend():** Where .lag() is like the .prevmember function, .lend is like .nextmember. A .lend function with a negative index is like a .lag() function.

- **.firstchild:** The .firstchild returns the first child under a parent.

  The first child under the Bottles and Cages subcategory is Mountain Bottle Cage.

  [Product].[Product Categories].[Subcategory].&[28].firstchild

- **.lastchild:** Just like .firstchild function returns the first child, .lastchild returns the last child under a parent.

  The last child under the Bottles and Cages subcategory is Water Bottle - 30 oz.

  [Product].[Product Categories].[Subcategory].&[28].lastchild

- **Ancestor:** The Ancestor function returns a single member at a given level or for a given distance, the number of level to go up.

  The ancestor for the Road Bottle Cage product in the Product Categories hierarchy at the Category level is Accessories.

```
Ancestor([Product].[Product Categories].[Product].&[479],
[Product].[Product Categories].[Category])
```

If we want to know the ancestor two levels above the `Road Bottle Cage` product in the `Product Categories` hierarchy, you would write:

```
Ancestor([Product].[Product Categories].[Product].&[479], 2)
```

- **Descendants:** The `Descendants` function takes two arguments. The first one is the member. The second argument is either a level name or a distance, just like the `Ancestor` function. The third argument is the flag to specify what to get and how to get it. The possible values for the third argument are: SELF, AFTER, BEFORE, BEFORE_AND_AFTER, SELF_AND_AFTER, SELF_AND_BEFORE, SELF_BEFORE_AFTER, and LEAVES.

  The descendants of the `Accessories` category in the `Product Categories` hierarchy in the `Product` dimension, at the subcategory level are: `Bike Racks`, `Bike Stands`, `Bottles and Cages`, `Cleaners`, `Fenders`, `Helmets`, `Hydration Packs`, `Lights`, `Locks`, `Panniers`, `Pumps`, `Tires`, and `Tubes`. The SELF flag is the default flag for the third argument.

  ```
  Descendants([Product].[Product Categories].[Category].&[4],
  [Product].[Product Categories].[Subcategory], SELF)
  ```

  Using the AFTER flag, you will get all the products under the subcategories of the `Accessories` category.

  ```
  Descendants([Product].[Product Categories].[Category].&[4],
  [Product].[Product Categories].[Subcategory], AFTER)
  ```

  The SELF_AND_AFTER flag will give you the subcategories and the products under the `Accessories` category.

  ```
  Descendants([Product].[Product Categories].[Category].&[4],
  [Product].[Product Categories].[Subcategory], SELF_AND_AFTER)
  ```

  With the BEFORE flag, you will get the `Accessories` category.

  ```
  Descendants([Product].[Product Categories].[Category].&[4],
  [Product].[Product Categories].[Subcategory], BEFORE)
  ```

  With the SELF_AND_BEFORE flag, you will get the `Accessories` category and the subcategories under `Accessories`.

  ```
  Descendants([Product].[Product Categories].[Category].&[4],
  [Product].[Product Categories].[Subcategory], SELF_AND_BEFORE)
  ```

  BEFORE_AND_AFTER returns the `Accessories` category with all the products under it, skipping the subcategories.

  ```
  Descendants([Product].[Product Categories].[Category].&[4],
  [Product].[Product Categories].[Subcategory], BEFORE_AND_AFTER)
  ```

SELF_BEFORE_AFTER gets the Accessories category with all the subcateogries and the products under it.

```
Descendants([Product].[Product Categories].[Category].&[4],
[Product].[Product Categories].[Subcategory], SELF_BEFORE_AFTER)
```

The LEAVES flag returns the leaf members.

```
Descendants([Product].[Product Categories].[Category].&[4],
[Product].[Product Categories].[Subcategory], LEAVES)
```

Can you spare the time?

In the vast majority of cubes, the dimension that you will find almost every time, is the date dimension.

- ParallelPeriod: The ParallelPeriod lags for a specific level (the first argument), for a number of steps (the second argument), and starts for a member (the third argument).

  So, ParallelPeriod([Date].[Calendar].[Month], 4, [Date].[Calendar].[Month].&[2008]&[2]) means that starts at February 2008, and go back four months ago. It will return October 2007. Enter a negative number to lead instead of lag. ParallelPeriod([Date].[Calendar].[Month], -4, [Date].[Calendar].[Month].&[2008]&[2]) returns June 2008.

- YTD: The YTD function returns a set containing all the members from the first one up to a specified member for the year of the member in the argument.

  YTD([Date].[Calendar].[Month].&[2008]&[5]) returns the months of January to May for the year 2008.

- QTD: The QTD function returns a set containing all the members from the first one up to a specified member for the quarter of the member in the argument.

  QTD([Date].[Calendar].[Month].&[2008]&[5]) returns the months April and May for the year 2008. The second Quarter of 2008 contains the months of April, May and June. Since May is entered, only April and May are returned.

- MTD: The MTD function returns all the members from the first one to the one specified in the given month.

  MTD([Date].[Calendar].[Date].&[20061027]) returns from October 1st to October 27th.

- WTD: The WTD function returns all the members from the first one to the one specified in the given week.

- LastPeriods: The LastPeriods function returns a set of a number of periods, the first argument, at the current level of the specified member, the 2nd argument.

  LastPeriods(4, [Date].[Calendar].[Month].&[2006]&[10]) returns a set from July 2006 to October 2006.

- **OpeningPeriod**: The `OpeningPeriod` function returns the first member at a given level for a specific member.

    `OpeningPeriod([Date].[Calendar].[Calendar Quarter], [Date].[Calendar].[Calendar Year].&[2006])` returns `Q1 CY 2006`, the first quarter for the year 2006.

- **ClosingPeriod**: The `ClosingPeriod` function is like the `OpeningPeriod` function, but returns the last member instead of the first one.

    `ClosingPeriod([Date].[Calendar].[Calendar Quarter], [Date].[Calendar].[Calendar Year].&[2006])` returns `Q4 CY 2006`, the last quarter for the year 2006.

Using Calculated Members and Named Sets

When you want to calculate your own measures, you have to define them as **Calculated Members**. Instead of repeating a set over and over again, use **Named Sets**.

Calculated Members

If you want to know the number of Order Count, Internet Order Count, and Non-Internet Order Count per Product Category for 2008, you will have to write this query using a `WITH` section. The Non-Internet Order Count measure is defined like this: `with member [Measures].[Non-Internet Order Count] as [Measures].[Order Count] - [Measures].[Internet Order Count]`. Then, in your Measures axe, add `[Measures].[Non-Internet Order Count]`.

The query will look like this:

```
with
member [Measures].[Non-Internet Order Count] as
[Measures].[Order Count] - [Measures].[Internet Order Count]

select {[Measures].[Order Count], [Measures].[Internet Order Count],
[Measures].[Non-Internet Order Count]} on 0,
[Product].[Category].[Category].members on 1
from [adventure works] where [Date].[Calendar].[Calendar Year].&[2008]
```

Here is the result of the Non-Internet Order Count:

	Order Count	Internet Order Count	Non-Internet Order Count
Accessories	10,950	10,657	293
Bikes	6,529	5,805	724
Clothing	5,012	4,451	561
Components	601	(null)	601

If you want to add more calculated members, only a single `WITH` keyword is required:

```
with

member [Measures].[Non-Internet Order Count] as
[Measures].[Order Count] - [Measures].[Internet Order Count]

member [Measures].[Non-Internet Order Count Ratio] as
[Measures].[Non-Internet Order Count] / [Measures].[Order Count]

select {[Measures].[Order Count], [Measures].[Internet Order Count],
[Measures].[Non-Internet Order Count], [Measures].[Non-Internet Order
Count Ratio]} on 0,
[Product].[Category].[Category].members on 1
from [adventure works] where [Date].[Calendar].[Calendar Year].&[2008]
```

Here is the result of the Non-Internet Order Count Ratio:

	Order Count	Internet Order Count	Non-Internet Order Count	Non-Internet Order Count Ratio
Accessories	10,950	10,657	293	2.67579908675799E-02
Bikes	6,529	5,805	724	0.110889875938122
Clothing	5,012	4,451	561	0.111931364724661
Components	601	(null)	601	1

The Non-Internet Order Count Ratio is a percentage, but it is not displayed like this. To change this, we use the `format_string` property at the end of the measure:

```
with

member [Measures].[Non-Internet Order Count] as
[Measures].[Order Count] - [Measures].[Internet Order Count]

member [Measures].[Non-Internet Order Count Ratio] as
[Measures].[Non-Internet Order Count] / [Measures].[Order Count]
, format_string="Percent"

select {[Measures].[Order Count], [Measures].[Internet Order Count],
[Measures].[Non-Internet Order Count], [Measures].[Non-Internet Order
Count Ratio]} on 0,
[Product].[Category].[Category].members on 1
from [adventure works] where [Date].[Calendar].[Calendar Year].&[2008]
```

Here is the new result with the Non-Internet Order Count Ratio formatted as a percentage:

	Order Count	Internet Order Count	Non-Internet Order Count	Non-Internet Order Count Ratio
Accessories	10,950	10,657	293	2.68%
Bikes	6,529	5,805	724	11.09%
Clothing	5,012	4,451	561	11.19%
Components	601	(null)	601	100.00%

Named Sets

Named Sets are sets that you can reference, so you can use them more than once in your query. Named Sets are written after the `WITH` keyword at the beginning of your MDX query. So under a `WITH` keyword, you can define a calculated member and two Named Sets, and end with another Calculated Members before starting writing the `SELECT` clause.

```
with
set [JanuaryToJune2008] as YTD([Date].[Calendar].[Month].&[2008]&[6])
member [Measures].[Order Count YTD] as sum(YTD([Date].[Calendar].
currentmember), [Measures].[Order Count])

select {[Measures].[Order Count], [Measures].[Order Count YTD]} on 0,
[JanuaryToJune2008] on 1
from [adventure works] where [Product].[Category].&[1]
```

Here is the result of the Order Count YTD for the Bikes from January to June 2008:

	Order Count	Order Count YTD
January 2008	860	860
February 2008	990	1,850
March 2008	1,021	2,871
April 2008	1,048	3,919
May 2008	1,280	5,199
June 2008	1,330	6,529

Calculations

When you use Calculated Members and Named Sets in your queries, you will use them over and over. Instead of repeating yourself in multiple MDX queries, you write the Calculated Members and the Named Sets inside your cube.

The calculation tab

Here is the procedure to display the cube's calculations:

1. Open the solution of your cube.
2. Once the solution opened, in the **Solution Explorer** window, expand the **Cubes** node, and double-click on your cube.
3. Click on the **Calculations** tab.

Add a new Calculated Member

Follow this procedure to add a new Calculated Member in your cube:

1. From the **Calculations** tab, click on the **New Calculated Member** button.
2. Enter a name for the Calculated Member.
3. In the **Expression** textbox, type the expression; the part after the AS when you write Calculated Members in a MDX query in SSMS.
4. Change the format string accordingly.
5. Right-click on the cube and click on **Process**.
6. Follow the instructions to process the cube.

    Here is a screenshot of the `[Measures].[Non-Internet Order Count Ratio]` measure in the **Calculations** tab:

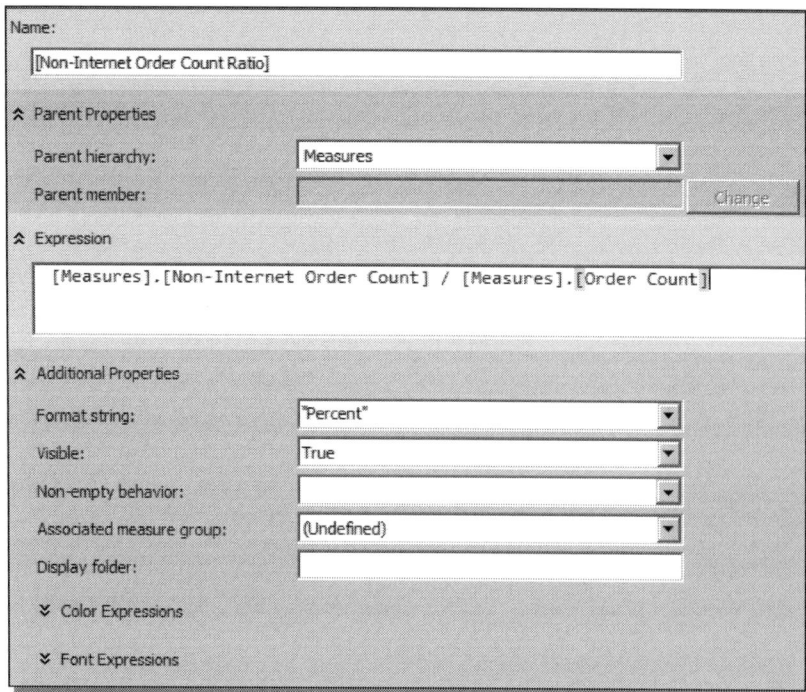

Add a new Named Set

Follow this procedure to add a new Named Set in your cube.

1. From the **Calculations** tab, click on the **New Named Set** button.
2. Enter a name for the Named Set.
3. In the **Expression** textbox, type the expression; the part after the AS when you write Named Sets in a MDX query in SSMS.
4. Right-click on the cube and click on **Process**.
5. Follow the instructions to process the cube.

   Here is a screenshot of the **[JanuaryToJune2008]** Named Set:

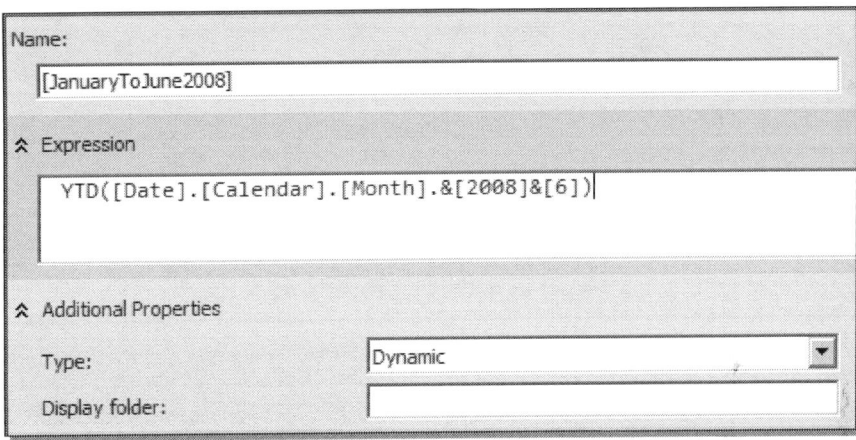

Then, when your Calculated Members and Named Sets are defined in your cube, you can refer them directly in your MDX query without redefining them in the WITH section.

```
select {[Measures].[Order Count], [Measures].[Internet Order Count],
[Measures].[Non-Internet Order Count], [Measures].[Non-Internet Order
Count Ratio]} on 0,
[Product].[Category].[Category].members on 1
from [adventure works] where [Date].[Calendar].[Calendar Year].&[2008]
```

Writing for SSRS

Once you know how to write the MDX queries, the result of your query in the grid in SSMS aren't useful to end users. A good way to show the numbers is to use the SQL Server Reporting Services or SSRS. With SSRS, you can create list, tables, matrices, and graphs. The first step to write reports is to create an SSRS project.

Create a Report Project

Follow this procedure to create a SQL Server Reporting Services Report Project:

1. Click on **Start** | **All Programs** | **Microsoft SQL Server 2012** and then **SQL Server Data Tools**.
2. Click on **File** and then **New Project**.
3. In the **Installed Templates** panel on the left, expand **Business Intelligence**, and then click on **Reporting Services**.
4. Select **Report Server Project**.
5. Type a **Name** for your project and select a **Location**.
6. Click on **OK**.

Create a new report

Once you have created your project, create a report:

1. In the **Solution Explorer** window on the right, right-click on the **Reports** folder and click on **Add** and then click on **New Item**.
2. Select **Report**.
3. Type a **Name** for your new report and then click on **Add**.

Create a data source

Now that you have a report, you have to create a data source to connect on your cube:

1. In the **Report Data** tab, right-click on **Data Sources** and then click on **Add Data Source**.
2. In the left panel, click on **General**.
3. Type a **Name** for your data source.
4. Select **Embedded connection**.
5. Change the **Type** to **Microsoft SQL Server Analysis Services**.
6. Click on **Edit**.
7. Type the **Server name** of the cube.
8. In the **Connect to a database** section, select **database**.
9. Select **AdventureWorksDW2012Multidimensional-EE**.
10. Click on **Test Connection** to verify if the test succeeded and then click on **OK**.
11. Click on **OK**.
12. In the left panel, click on **Credentials**.

13. Select **Use Windows Authentication (integrated security)**.
14. Click on **OK**.

Create a dataset

With a data source configured on your cube, you can add one or more dataset in your report. Dataset is where you write a MDX query so that the SSRS report will display the result in a list, table, matrix, and/or graph.

1. In the **Report Data** tab, right-click on **Datasets** and then click on **Add Dataset**.
2. Type a **Name** for your dataset.
3. Select **Use a dataset embedded in my report**.
4. Select the data source created previously.
5. Click on **Query Designer**.
6. Click on the **Design Mode** button to switch the designer in text mode.
7. Write your MDX query.
8. Click on **Execute Query** to view the result.
9. Click on **OK**.
10. Click on **OK**.

Here is the print screen of the result in the Query Designer of the following MDX query:

```
with
set [Months] as YTD([Date].[Calendar].[Month].&[2008]&[6])
member [Measures].[Order Count YTD] as sum(YTD([Date].[Calendar].
currentmember), [Measures].[Order Count])

select {[Measures].[Order Count], [Measures].[Order Count YTD]} on 0,
[Months] on 1
from [adventure works] where [Product].[Category].&[1]
```

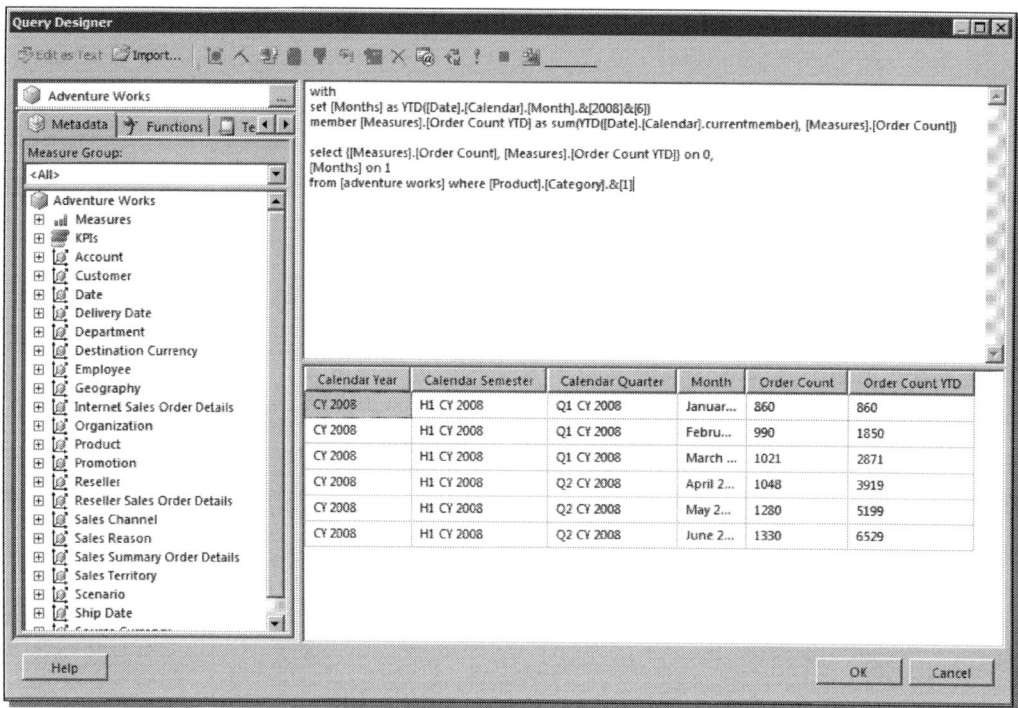

Once the dataset is created, you have access to the fields of the dataset from the **Report Data** tab.

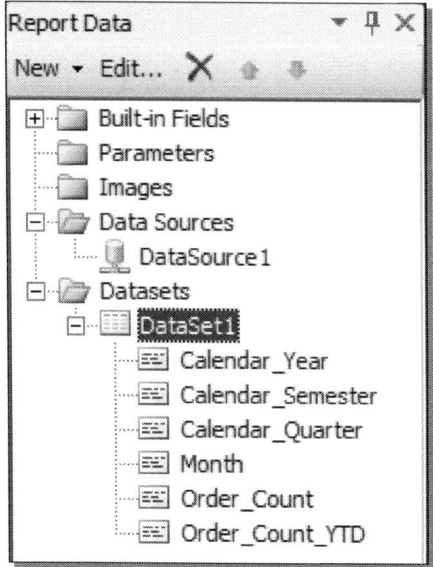

Create a table

Add a table to display the information from the dataset as follows:

1. In the **Toolbar**, click on **Table** report item and then drag it in the **Report Body**.
2. In the **Table** report item, click on the left-most cell at the bottom of the table.
3. Click on the **Field** button and select **Month**.
4. Click on the cell next to the right and select **Order_Count**.
5. Click on the cell next to the right and select **Order_Count_YTD**.
6. Adjust the width of the columns.
7. Click on the **Preview** tab to see a preview of your report.

The table in the Design mode with the **Field** menu displayed as follows:

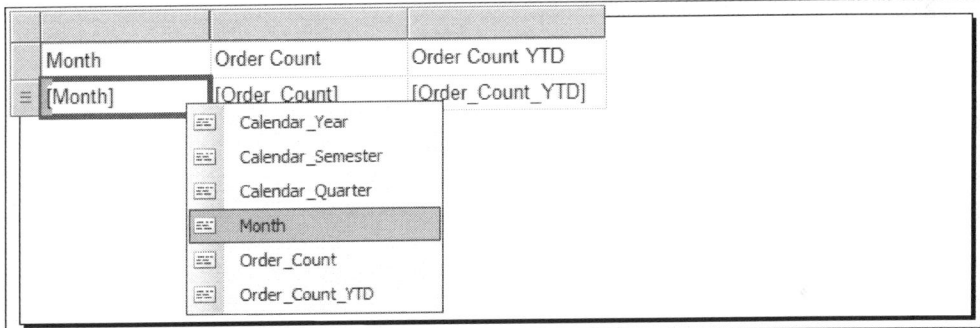

The table in the Preview mode is as follows:

Month	Order Count	Order Count YTD
January 2008	860	860
February 2008	990	1850
March 2008	1021	2871
April 2008	1048	3919
May 2008	1280	5199
June 2008	1330	6529

 Once in a while, the **Report Data** tab is missing when you open your SSRS project. To show up the toolbox, click on **View** and then **Report Data** or press *Ctrl + Alt + D*.

The Months parameter

The `Report` parameters can give the user the ability to select the filter values they want to have for their reports. To use a parameter with the values from a cube, you will have to:

- Create a new dataset
- Add a new parameter
- Change the query from the first dataset to take the parameter value

Create a new dataset and enter the following query to get the months from 2006 to 2008:

```
with
member [Measures].[Label] as [Date].[Calendar].currentmember.member_caption
member [Measures].[Value] as [Date].[Calendar].currentmember.unique_name
select {[Measures].[Label], [Measures].[Value]} on 0, [Date].
[Calendar].[Month].members on 1
from [adventure works]
where [Date].[Calendar Year].&[2006] : [Date].[Calendar Year].&[2008]
```

Take note of two functions, `.member_caption` and `.unique_name`. `.member_caption` displays the name of the member and `.unique_name` returns the unique name with the keys of the member used by SSAS.

	Label	Value
January 2006	January 2006	[Date].[Calendar].[Month].&[2006]&[1]
February 2006	February 2006	[Date].[Calendar].[Month].&[2006]&[2]
March 2006	March 2006	[Date].[Calendar].[Month].&[2006]&[3]
...	...	...

When you have configured the parameter's dataset, add a parameter to the report:

1. In the **Report Data** tab, right-click on the **Parameters** folder and click on **Add Parameter**.
2. Type a **Name** and a **Prompt** for the parameter.
3. In the left panel, click on **Available Values**.
4. Click on **Get values from a query**.
5. Select the dataset containing the months.
6. Select a **Value field** and a **Label** field.
7. Click on **OK**.

Here is a screenshot of the Month parameter:

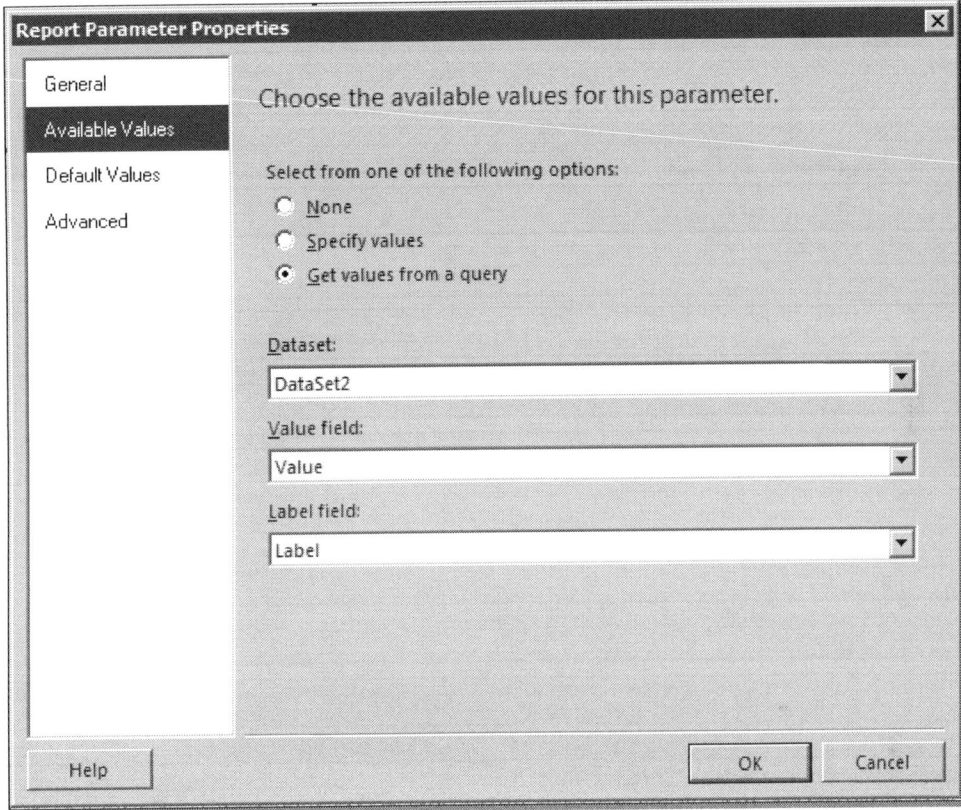

When you have configured a report parameter, change the query of the first dataset to include the parameter value:

1. Right-click on the first dataset created and click on **Dataset Properties**.
2. On the left menu, click on **Parameters**.
3. Click on **Add**.
4. Type Month for the **Parameter Name** and select [@Month] for the **Parameter Value**.
5. In the left menu, click on **Query**.
6. Click on **Query Designer**.
7. Replace in the MDX query, [Date].[Calendar].[Month].&[2008]&[6], with STRTOMEMBER(@Month).
8. Click on the **Query Parameters** button.
9. In the Parameter type Month, select the **Date** dimension and the Date.Calendar hierarchy, and set the default value to **October 2008**.

10. Click on **OK**.
11. Click on **Execute Query**.
12. Click on **OK**.
13. Click on **OK**.
14. Right-click on the **@Month** parameter.
15. Click on **Default Values** on the left panel.
16. Select **No default value**.
17. Click on **OK**.

The **Query Parameters** window is as follows:

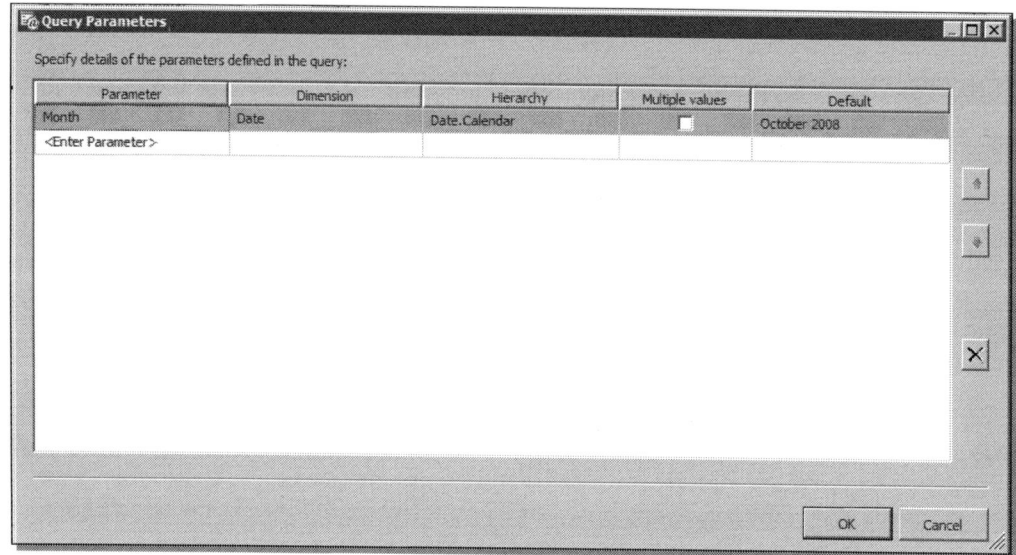

Follow this procedure to preview the report:

1. Click on the **Preview** tab.
2. On the top of the report, select a **Month** and then click on **View Report** on the right.

Here is a screenshot of the report for October 2007:

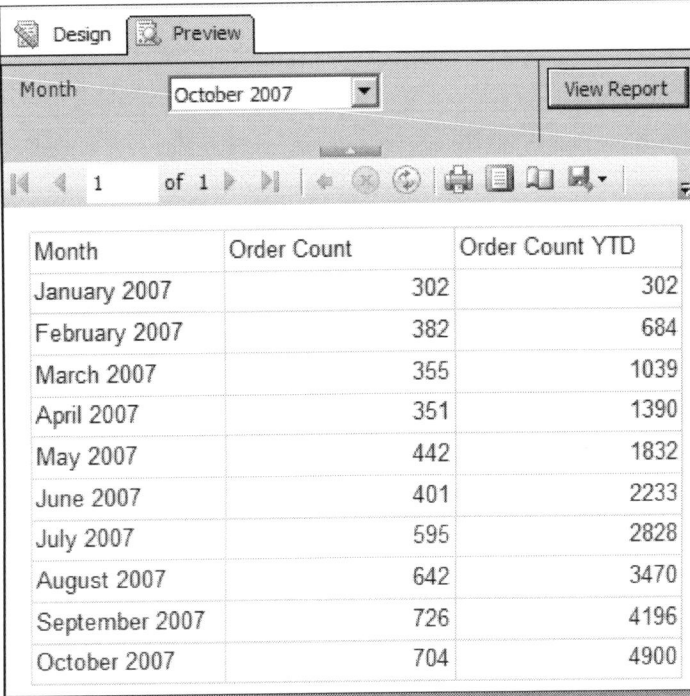

DMVs

Whenever you want to have a quick look at the cube documentation such as the star schemas or the bus matrix, use SSAS exposes **Dynamic Management Views**.

1. To see the list of DMVs available, execute the following query in a **MDX query** window in SSMS:

   ```
   SELECT * FROM $System.DBSCHEMA_TABLES
   WHERE TABLE_SCHEMA = '$SYSTEM'
   ```

2. If you want to identify the measures in your cube, query the $System.MDSCHEMA_MEASURES DMV:

   ```
   SELECT * FROM $System.MDSCHEMA_MEASURES
   WHERE CUBE_NAME = 'Adventure Works'
   ```

3. The `$System.MDSCHEMA_MEASUREGROUP_DIMENSIONS` DVM provides where the dimensions meets the measure groups in the cube. With this, you can document your star schemas and bus matrix.

   ```
   SELECT * FROM $System.MDSCHEMA_MEASUREGROUP_DIMENSIONS
   WHERE CUBE_NAME = 'Adventure Works'
   ```

4. For details about dimensions, use `MDSCHEMA_DIMENSIONS`.

   ```
   SELECT * FROM $System.MDSCHEMA_DIMENSIONS
   WHERE CUBE_NAME = 'Adventure Works'
   ```

For a complete list of SSAS DMVs, go to http://msdn.microsoft.com/en-us/library/ms126212.aspx for the OLE DB Schema rowsets (DBSCHEMA) and http://msdn.microsoft.com/en-us/library/ms126079.aspx for the OLE DB OLAP Schema rowsets (MDSCHEMA). With this, I can build a query to have my cube documentation real-time with a few clicks.

People and places you should get to know

If you need help with the MDX Queries for SQL Server 2012, here are some people and places which will prove invaluable:

Official Sites

Homepage: http://www.microsoft.com/en-us/sqlserver/default.aspx

Manual and documentation: http://msdn.microsoft.com/en-US/sqlserver/

Articles and Tutorials

Tutorial for Multidimensional Modeling, a must if you have to start you journey with SSAS cubes before learning MDX:
http://technet.microsoft.com/en-us/library/db55e226-601a-4026-8651-573195555a59

Key Concepts in MDX, SSAS terminology:
http://msdn.microsoft.com/en-us/library/ms144884.aspx

MDX Query Fundamentals, more information on the basic MDX query, calculation and named sets:
http://msdn.microsoft.com/en-us/library/ms145514.aspx

SQLBI, the website of Marco Russo and Alberto Ferrari: http://www.sqlbi.com/

Kimball Group, a good MDX query starts with a good data warehouse architecture:
http://www.kimballgroup.com/

Blogs

The blog of Marco Russo: http://sqlblog.com/blogs/marco_russo/

The blog of Alberto Ferrari: http://sqlblog.com/blogs/alberto_ferrari/

The blog of Chris Webb: http://cwebbbi.wordpress.com/

The blog of James Serra: http://www.jamesserra.com

The blog of Nicholas Emond (niko 2 point zero): http://niko2point0.wordpress.com/

Twitter

Follow Marco Russo on Twitter: `https://twitter.com/marcorus`

Follow Alberto Ferrari on Twitter: `https://twitter.com/FerrariAlberto`

Follow Chris Webb on Twitter: `https://twitter.com/Technitrain`

Follow James Serra on Twitter: `https://twitter.com/JamesSerra`

Follow Nicholas Emond on Twitter: `https://twitter.com/nicholasemond`

For more Open Source information, follow Packt at `http://twitter.com/#!/packtopensource`

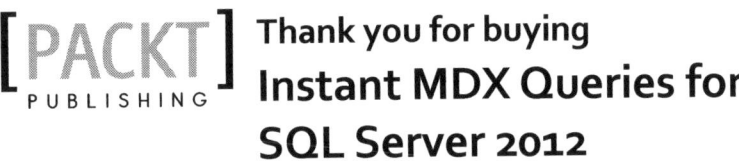

Thank you for buying
Instant MDX Queries for SQL Server 2012

About Packt Publishing

Packt, pronounced 'packed', published its first book "*Mastering phpMyAdmin for Effective MySQL Management*" in April 2004 and subsequently continued to specialize in publishing highly focused books on specific technologies and solutions.

Our books and publications share the experiences of your fellow IT professionals in adapting and customizing today's systems, applications, and frameworks. Our solution based books give you the knowledge and power to customize the software and technologies you're using to get the job done. Packt books are more specific and less general than the IT books you have seen in the past. Our unique business model allows us to bring you more focused information, giving you more of what you need to know, and less of what you don't.

Packt is a modern, yet unique publishing company, which focuses on producing quality, cutting-edge books for communities of developers, administrators, and newbies alike. For more information, please visit our website: www.packtpub.com.

Writing for Packt

We welcome all inquiries from people who are interested in authoring. Book proposals should be sent to author@packtpub.com. If your book idea is still at an early stage and you would like to discuss it first before writing a formal book proposal, contact us; one of our commissioning editors will get in touch with you.

We're not just looking for published authors; if you have strong technical skills but no writing experience, our experienced editors can help you develop a writing career, or simply get some additional reward for your expertise.

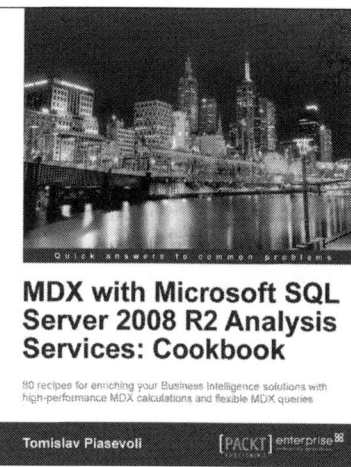

MDX with Microsoft SQL Server 2008 R2 Analysis Services Cookbook

ISBN: 978-1-84968-130-8 Paperback: 480 pages

80 recipes for enriching your Business Intelligence solutions with high-performance MDX calculations and flexible MDX queries

1. Enrich your BI solutions by implementing best practice MDX calculations
2. Master a wide range of time-related, context-aware, and business-related calculations
3. Enhance your solutions by combining MDX with utility dimensions

MDX with SSAS 2012 Cookbook

ISBN: 978-1-84968-960-1 Paperback: 542 pages

Over 90 practical recipes to analyze multidimensional data stored in SSAS 2012 cubes, using high-performance MDX calculations and flexible MDX queries

1. A wide range of time-related, context-aware, and business-related calculations
2. Combine MDX with utility dimensions
3. Illustration of techniques to enrich business intelligence solutions, aided by practical, hands-on Cookbook recipes

Please check **www.PacktPub.com** for information on our titles

Microsoft SQL Server 2012 Performance Tuning Cookbook

ISBN: 978-1-84968-574-0   Paperback: 478 pages

80 recipes to help you tune SQL Server 2012 and achieve optimal performance

1. Learn about the performance tuning needs for SQL Server 2012 with this book and ebook
2. Diagnose problems when they arise and employ tricks to prevent them
3. Explore various aspects that affect performance by following the clear recipes

Microsoft SQL Server 2012 Integration Services: An Expert Cookbook

ISBN: 978-1-84968-524-5   Paperback: 564 pages

Over 80 expert recipes to design, create, and deploy SSIS packages

1. Full of illustrations, diagrams, and tips with clear step-by-step instructions and real time examples
2. Master all transformations in SSIS and their usages with real-world scenarios
3. Learn to make SSIS packages re-startable and robust; and work with transactions

Please check **www.PacktPub.com** for information on our titles

Made in the USA
Lexington, KY
19 April 2015